P9-CIW-962

Decorating
for the
Holidays

Valerie Parr Hill

TEXT BY MARY CALDWELL

PHOTOGRAPHY BY JEFF MCNAMARA

QVC PUBLISHING, INC.

QVC Publishing, Inc.
Jill Cohen, Vice President and Publisher
Ellen Bruzelius, General Manager
Sarah Butterworth, Editorial Director
Cassandra Reynolds, Publishing Assistant

Produced by Smallwood & Stewart, Inc., New York City
Designer: Amy Henderson
Stylist: Ingrid Leess

Q Publishing and colophon
are trademarks of QVC Publishing, Inc.

Published by QVC Publishing, Inc., 50 Main Street,
Mount Kisco, New York 10549

Manufactured in Singapore

ISBN: 1-928998-35-6
Library of Congress catalogue information available on request.
First Edition

10 9 8 7 6 5 4 3 2 1

Foreword

THE SCENT OF BALSAM and the sight of a tree in the living room never fail to awaken fond Christmas memories for me. Each year, the holidays bring the pleasure of traditions revisited as well as the magic of today's special moments. I love the ritual of unwrapping our family's collection of ornaments and choosing spots for the visual and aromatic details that delight our senses and are firmly woven into holiday memories.

I ALSO REALIZE THAT THE FESTIVE FRENZY of the holiday season can seem overwhelming when we wear ourselves out in pursuit of a picture-perfect holiday. With this book, I've gathered together some of my favorite easy decorating ideas to bring the holiday spirit home and still leave plenty of time to appreciate and enjoy the true meaning of Thanksgiving and Christmas. After all, as we celebrate with family and friends, we are creating warm, comforting memories that will enrich our lives for years to come—and that's what makes a home truly beautiful.

HAPPY HOLIDAYS!

Valerie

Late November's brisk days bring a feast for the senses:
Crimson mingles with gold and russet; leaves crackle
and sweet spices perfume the air; home beckons

Gathering Together

T

THERE'S SOMETHING ABOUT AUTUMN that appeals to me more than any other time of year. Spring brings joy after a long winter, for sure, but nature's true brilliance stands out in fall. The momentary beauty is to be savored all the more for the certainty that the next hard rain will bring the glorious foliage to the ground. And so with great anticipation each year, I set about readying my home for the season and its high point at Thanksgiving, a holiday I dearly love. This season offers a wealth of decorating possibilities, often requiring little more than an artful gathering of natural treasures.

BEAUTY AND SIMPLICITY merge in a striking queue of acorn squash, pumpkins, and goose-neck squash, notable for the spectrum of fall colors and the intriguing contrast of ridged and smooth, round and bulbous.

AS THANKSGIVING'S ROOTS are so closely linked to the harvest, the best decorations come straight from nature, or at least take their inspiration from autumn's abundance of pumpkins, corn, squash, sheaves of wheat, chrysanthemums, all manner of nuts, colored leaves, berries. I love highlighting these seasonal "ingredients" in centerpiece arrangements at home because the mood they convey is so unforced and so congenial for family and visitors alike—which is, for me, the whole point of home decorating.

A CASUAL COLLAGE of squashes, pumpkins, mums, and apples on the front porch (OPPOSITE AND OVERLEAF) invites family and friends to relax and savor a golden fall day. My son Jeffrey has the task of selecting the perfect spot for hanging our bunch of Indian corn (ABOVE).

FOR FALL DECORATING, it's hard to top the colors, shapes, and textures of the various winter squash and gourds. Some squashes are sleek and smooth, like the tan butternut or the pale yellow spaghetti squash; other varieties, such as the Turk's turban, the gooseneck, or the warty, oversized Hubbard (possibly the "mother of all squashes," often weighing more than ten pounds!) are downright comical with their various stripes, knobby tops, or asymmetrical lumps and bumps. Gourds, traditional for fall decorating, come in shades of white, green, yellow, and orange; cooking enthusiasts may prefer to decorate with baskets of equally

picturesque but infinitely more edible diminutive squashes that have become readily available in the last decade or so, including miniature pumpkins, delicata, or sweet dumpling squash. These thick-skinned charmers fit into almost any decorating style, from country to formal.

A WARM WELCOME HOME

HOME IS WHERE WE SHOW love to those we care about most. I don't need or want to have the "fanciest" house around. My goal, always, is to create a warm and welcoming home, filled with things my family and I love, one that's both comfortable to live in and delightful to visit. Matching the mood of the home to the season plays an important part in all of this. I confess that I sometimes move too fast, distracted by competing demands on the limited number of hours in my day. But I find holiday decorating soothing, as it brings an opportunity to linger, if briefly, and appreciate a season that can seem all too fleeting. Fortunately, I've discovered that holiday decorating builds not from grand, sweeping displays, but from many small, beautiful touches, details that are often remarkably quick and easy to achieve.

BEING AWARE OF THE POWER of first impressions, I want my guests to feel welcome even before they set foot inside our house. The path and steps leading up to the front door, the front porch, and of course, the entry door itself are all blank canvases ready to be dressed up.

ANY SPOT AT ALL is fair game for dress-up in November, and even little touches can contribute immeasurably to the overall mood of celebration. Here, a branch of bittersweet snipped from a garden vine, is fastened to the porch lantern with a golden ribbon—very simple, so pretty!

Place a pair of large pumpkins to flank a front door. March a troop of pumpkins up the front steps, stretch a conga line of squash across a porch railing, or see how they provide colorful relief to a post-summer window box. In the corner of an old-fashioned porch or back deck, mix and match baskets of squash, piles of pumpkins, and a pot or two of chrysanthemums or some dried flowers.

Don't be afraid to mix up the palette. As much as I love and take advantage of autumn's traditional gold-red-orange scheme, it can be fun—and dramatic—to play with unconventional color combinations. A blue bench looks lovely as the backdrop for a group of squashes and pumpkins—like the November sky above a canopy of leaves. Or introduce purple to an autumn vignette; it can really make the golden fall colors "pop."

POTPOURRI on an entry table (ABOVE) keeps company with a moss-filled urn. Because the urn is deep, I first filled it halfway with lightweight packing peanuts.

A MIRROR brings another "window" into a room (OPPOSITE). The decorative wreath includes lifelike apples and pears and eucalyptus in natural and dyed hues. The off-center candle adds visual interest.

SCENTS OF THE HOLIDAYS

WHILE SETTING THE MOOD for the season relies heavily on the visual, aromas can also play a key role. Fragrances trigger powerful emotions and memories; a pleasant aroma when you walk through the front door will instantly put you at ease, letting you know that warm hospitality awaits. Among the most enticing, of course, are the delicious aromas of the

(continued on page 31)

CANDLELIT HOLIDAYS

Did candlelight seem so romantic in the days before people had incandescent, or worse, fluorescent lights for comparison? The golden glow, ever changing as the flames flicker, is an integral part of the holidays for me. I love candles and the way they can transform the mood of a room, from the formal elegance of tapers in silver holders to the chubby cheer of squat pillar candles on a mantel or casual supper table. I'll even set candles in traditional luminarias or a bucket of sand or water by the front porch to welcome guests.

To prolong burning and symmetry of shape, plan the candle's debut to allow it to burn uninterrupted for one hour per inch of diameter (that is, a three-inch-diameter candle should burn initially for three hours) so the pool of melted wax extends out to the edges. This helps the candle to burn down evenly, without leaving a central hollow core surrounded by thick wax sides. Then, after you blow out the candle, use your fingers to mold the top outer edge of the still-warm candle gently towards the center.

Go ahead and burn those special holiday candles. The beauty, the life of a candle comes from its flame. Unused candles won't rust, true, but eventually colors fade (especially if the candle has been displayed in direct sunlight) and the wax may sag. To clean a candle that's become dusty, wipe it with a clean cloth moistened with a bit of mineral oil or cool water.

AN AUTUMN BERRY WREATH encircling a candle (OPPOSITE) heightens the seasonal ambience and makes a nice counterpoint to the tableau of pumpkins and winter squash on the sideboard.

SCENTED WITH vanilla buttercream, a trio of square candles smells as wonderful as it looks in its low, wrought-iron holder with scrolled sides and a braided rim (OVERLEAF). A pair of these holders, stair-step fashion, makes a unique dining table centerpiece. After blowing out the candles, trim the wicks so pieces won't break off when you next light them and mar the pure color of the wax.

THE FAMILY TABLE

As we gather together with family once again for Thanksgiving dinner, my husband, Will, and I are grateful for so much more than the fabulous meal that gets turned out every year. We are very aware that today's love and laughter will become the memories of our boys, Gene Colyer and Jeffrey. These comforting thoughts they will carry through their lives; then, when it's time, years from now, to create new memories with their own wives and children, they will be inspired by their holidays past—just as I keep always in my heart the warm, lively Thanksgiving dinners of my Kentucky childhood.

That's why I love dressing up the table, where the day's main event unfolds, so that all present will know that they are a very special part of the day and that we are so glad to have them with us. I rarely choose expansive centerpieces; I find they block people's faces and interfere with conversations. Instead, I prefer to scatter smaller seasonal elements the length of the table. A cloth runner laid down the center goes a long way toward unifying the assortment of pumpkins, gourds, and leaves that Jeff and Gene rambunctiously gather outside early that morning. Sometimes I'll scatter a few acorns or walnuts, too. A votive candle in a glass holder marks each place, diffusing the flattering glow of candlelight shining on the group of dear, happy faces.

OUR OWN YARD supplies us with autumn oak leaves to decorate the Thanksgiving table (OPPOSITE). Some years, my mother sends us delicate lacy leaves from the sweet gum trees at home in Kentucky. She presses them between sheets of waxed paper so they'll keep their color.

I LOVE TO SERVE my Thanksgiving soup (BELOW) with a simple heart-shaped garnish of pita bread stamped out with a cookie cutter, circled by fresh parsley.

GRANDMILLIE'S PUMPKIN CHIFFON PIE

One secret of a terrific Thanksgiving: belong to a family of great bakers! My sister-in-law Mary specializes in heavenly apple pies; the superb pumpkin chiffon below comes from Will's mother, Mildred—"Grandmillie" to our boys. In my childhood, Aunt Pauline baked excellent pumpkin pies, and no Thanksgiving was complete unless Uncle Kearney managed to "snitch" an entire pie, which he would triumphantly brandish out the car window as he drove away!

3 large egg yolks

1 cup granulated sugar

1¼ cups cooked or canned pumpkin

½ cup milk

½ tsp. cinnamon

½ tsp. ground ginger

½ tsp. ground nutmeg

½ tsp. salt

2 tsps. gelatin soaked in ¼ cup cold water for 5 minutes

3 Tbsps. powdered egg white mixed with 6 Tbsps. water

1 prebaked pie shell

Whipped cream

1. In a large bowl with an electric mixer on high speed, beat the egg yolks with ½ cup sugar until well combined and light yellow. Add the pumpkin, milk, and spices and mix well, scraping down the sides of the bowl.
2. Transfer the mixture to a double boiler over gently simmering water and cook, stirring constantly until the mixture is thick, 10 to 12 minutes. Add the gelatin, stirring constantly until it is completely dissolved. Remove from the double boiler and cool.
3. In the large bowl of an electric mixer on high speed, beat the powdered egg white mixture and the remaining ½ cup sugar until stiff and glossy peaks form, about 5 minutes.
4. When the pumpkin mixture is cool and starting to thicken, use a rubber spatula to gently fold in the egg white mixture. Pour the filling into the pie shell. Cover with plastic wrap and chill for at least 4 hours, or overnight. Before serving, garnish with dollops of whipped cream.

SERVES 8 TO 10

WILL LAST 3 DAYS REFRIGERATED

RED AND GOLDEN APPLE CANDLES floating in a tin bucket by the front porch, welcome guests (LEFT). I still remember bobbing for apples when I was a Brownie scout—though my recollections seem to be mostly about giggles and dripping hair rather than actually capturing the fruit in my teeth!

THE WEATHERED WOOD of a barn door (OPPOSITE) lends rustic contrast to a wreath that showcases autumn's bounty, including dried oak leaves, lifelike miniature fruits and vegetables, and genuine pheasant feathers.

(continued from page 20)

Thanksgiving kitchen—turkey roasting, nutmeg and ginger as the apple and pumpkin pies bake, fresh-brewed coffee that accompanies dessert—but you do have other possibilities, too. Scented candles are one of my favorites, both for their own pleasant fragrance and for the way they seem to purify the air. If it's not your turn to make the pies, a simmer pot (or an improvised version made by sprinkling ground cinnamon and cloves into a saucepan of simmering water on the stove) can mimic the allure of sweet baked goods. A fragrant wreath—of eucalyptus, for example—hung inside the front door emits a pleasant scent every time the door is opened; a bowl of potpourri in the entry can be lovely, too. Whether you make your own potpourri from foraged treasures or purchase a packaged blend, you may find that the fragrance eventually fades, or that you wish to modify it slightly with another scent. You can revive the aroma from time to time with essential oils (available at craft shops), which come in small bottles that are often fitted with a dropper top. Add the oil sparingly—it should only take a drop or two—and stir gently to incorporate the oil uniformly. Your goal is to keep the potpourri subtly pleasant, not overpowering.

NEW LOOKS

WHILE I DO ADD NEW CANDLES and other pretty accessories to my personal collection each year, I like to find everyday things that will lend themselves, as is or with a minimal dress-up, to the seasonal theme. Colorful tin buckets or painted clay pots brought in from the garden might be just right for holding flowers. Or maybe simply grouping items that aren't usually displayed together—for example, silver-framed photographs with an urn of acorns—set on a colored fabric square and accompanied by a candle or mini pumpkin, will pull the look together. Do you have a pitcher that's on permanent display in the living room? Dress it up for the holidays by filling it with dried flowers or grasses and a feather or two. Tie a russet or other harvest-colored ribbon around the handle. Everyday ivy and other ordinary house plants need little more than a candle or two, or a small branch of natural or silk leaves in the autumn palette, to bring in another subtle touch of the season.

TULIPS ARE NOW AVAILABLE nearly all year round, and still they are a delightful surprise for holiday decorating. This color—brilliant red—helps bridge the transition from Thanksgiving to Christmas, which is important to me. Our Christmas tree goes up the very day after Thanksgiving! Similarly, the candles inserted into an ivy topiary suggest a wreath. The secret elements in this display, small pronged candle holders, come from my local florist's back room. Though the holders are rarely on display in the showroom, most florists have a supply available for their own arrangements—just ask.

BACKYARD BEAUTY

DRIED HYDRANGEA, their burnished pink petals illuminated by the glow of a candlelit "cathedral," can last all winter (BELOW). Pick the hydrangea in fall only after the tiny floret at the center of each cluster has opened and dropped off. Strip the leaves, then set the stems in two inches of water. (Don't refill.)

A BUTTER-YELLOW BOWL of oranges and pinecones, surrounded by evergreens, segues from November to December (OPPOSITE).

City dwellers on the whole may not be so lucky, but most of us have at our doorsteps a wealth of natural treasures that are perfect for turning into decorative touches to help celebrate the holidays. Next time you're outdoors, be on the lookout for:

Pinecones, from teensy to grand — *Bittersweet, with orange berries amid the tangled vines* — *Pyracantha ("firethorn"), which resembles bay leaves in miniature, studded with clusters of glorious orange-colored fall berries. One year, Will crafted a stunning wreath by tucking pyracantha into a grapevine base, securing as necessary with wire* — *Acorns and other seasonal nuts* — *"Silver pennies" or "Lunaria" (also know as money plant) for its moonlike quality* — *Sage, an herb-garden late-stayer endowed with fragrant, gray-green velvety leaves on woody stalks, a must for seasoning the Thanksgiving turkey and stuffing (or "dressing" if you're from the South) and an intriguing accent for autumn decorating* — *Rose hips, which form on leggy bushes, but beware of thorns* — *Milkweed pods, cattails, sumac, marsh grass, and other attractive "weeds."*

Fresh balsam wreaths, cedar garlands, big red bows—
dressed for the holidays, the house heralds our
merry welcome to the Christmas season

A Warm, Festive Home

W

WRAPPING UP THE HOUSE as if it were a giant present is what I think of when I begin planning which doors, windows, and railings will be hung with wreaths, graced with garlands, or circled with lights. Although I love seasonal decorating throughout the year, I pull out all the stops at Christmas, steadily building the family's anticipation for this favorite holiday. At our house, we begin decorating the day after Thanksgiving so we can enjoy the season's beauty for as long as possible. As the weeks pass, we continue to add decorative touches as time allows, and when inspiration strikes.

A CHEERY PATH of greenery—garlands, conifers in terra-cotta pots, ivy-blanketed topiaries, and lush wreaths accented with gold-trimmed red bows—is a fragrant approach to our front door. Welcome!

WE NEVER MISS AN OPPORTUNITY at this time of year to drive by and admire the most lavishly illuminated "Christmas House" in our neighborhood, though our own outdoor decorating is more low-key. We rely heavily on natural greenery—I always outline our porch railings with holiday garlands, and crown the windows with evergreen swags for a seasonal variation of the classic architectural pediment. There's the wreath for the front door, of course, and one on the front gate; why not the back door, the tool shed, the garage? Window wreaths can be enjoyed from inside or outside the house. To personalize purchased wreaths, fasten decorations from your own collection to the boughs with ribbon or wire. Bells on the front door wreath give a merry jingle every time the door opens. If there's a suitable space in the wreath's center, showcase a Christmas angel or a teddy bear with a little Santa hat or red ribbon bow tie.

THE FRONT PORCH is a good staging area for organizing greenery (OPPOSITE). At the ready are, clockwise from the basket, pinecones and berries, a balsam-juniper-cedar garland, holly, sheet moss, magnolia leaves, berry branches, and eucalyptus leaves.

HOLIDAY CHEER begins with a wreath on the front door and at the gate (ABOVE).

OUTSIDE, DELICATE GARLANDS can be looped around columns or scalloped down from a porch railing; very thick, full versions look better laid right on top. Wrap additional greenery in a spiral around lampposts.

CHRISTMAS IN EVERY CORNER

A DRAMATIC sweep of evergreen around the doorway is extra thick, to give the garland a full look. At the top center, a few sprigs of white berry have been wired into place. Not to be overlooked, the doorknob boasts its own evergreen and ribbon decoration; on Christmas day, I like to add one or two fresh roses to the doorknob decoration.

INSIDE THE HOUSE, it's amazing how windows, mirror frames, and doorways—every little corner—can pop into the limelight when they're outlined in the spirit of the season. Lush wreaths and garlands are lovely, but even a modest sprig of holly brings joy. You can easily fashion your own garlands by using thin coated wire or flexible copper wire to attach evergreens to lengths of twine. Starting at the bottom, overlap the branches so each sprig conceals the wire fastening the sprig before. Mix trimmings from the Christmas tree with greenery from the yard or garden-shop purchases—balsam, fir, cedar, yew, juniper, holly. In fact, gathering greens at home is a great outdoor activity with children or grandchildren. Keep the pruning shears to yourself, but let youngsters pull a wagon or carry a basket full of greens. Remember, some greens are prickly; heavy gloves are a must. (We're all rushed at some point during the holidays. Ready-made garlands save time and take only minutes to tack in place.) A daily spritz of water with a plant mister will prolong the fresh color and suppleness of garlands in the house.

TO DRESS UP YOUR GARLANDS, wire in pinecones, berry sprigs, rosehips, and seedpods if you like the woodsy appeal of natural-colored materials. Or if you wish, include trimmings and ornaments with a bit of gold. Visit the craft store and check out their selection of gilded leaves, berry sprigs, thistles and seedpods, silk poinsettias, and other embellishments.

CURTAIN TIEBACKS improvised from fresh greenery, lifelike berries, silk poinsettias, velvet streamers, and pinecones on a flexible wire base sweep the curtains back from the window, letting in the last lingering light of the day (OPPOSITE).

TURNING AN OPEN DOORWAY into a dramatic holiday archway requires no sewing (LEFT). Just swag a length of fabric around the doorway, fastening at the corners with tacks that can be concealed with berries and pinecones that take the place of tassels.

DISPLAYING CARDS

Christmas cards are well loved for the connections they help us maintain with faraway family and friends and for their own intrinsic beauty. After enjoying the day's mail, my mother piles holiday cards into a beautiful basket for everyone to peruse at their leisure. I think of cards as belonging to a seasonal gallery, ready for display. In addition to lining them up on a mantel or shelf, you can:

Drape ribbon along a mantel, window, or wall. Clip cards to the line with spring-action clothespins. Let the kids help out by decorating wooden clothespins with paint or glitter. *Cover a large rectangle of plywood, foam board, or corrugated cardboard with holiday-print fabric. Crisscross ribbons lattice-style in front, fastening them behind the board with a staple or hot glue. Tuck your greeting cards behind the ribbons.* *Punch a hole in the corner of each card, attach a ribbon loop, and hang from the Christmas tree.* *Cover a folding screen with your favorite cards by gluing the backs to the screen. Add new cards each year.*

SHANTUNG SILK topped with angels, a bow, and greenery fills a vertical slice of wall and showcases some of my prettiest Christmas cards (OPPOSITE). A dab of hot glue or a pin holds each card in place.

AS CARDS ARRIVE, tuck them into loops of decorative wire wound around a column topped with clusters of red berries (BELOW).

WRAP, PLEASE

I KNOW THERE ARE PEOPLE who consider wrapping presents a chore and gladly take advantage of every department-store gift wrap counter. For me, though, thoughtfully wrapped gifts are one of the delights of the season; the beautiful exterior always sharpens anticipation for the present within. Christmas is for giving, and after we've spent time to choose the perfect gift, a gorgeous wrapping makes that special something even more wonderful. My family may poke fun at me for my elaborate packages—but they sure love receiving them!

SHIMMERY RIBBONS make a wrapped gift luxurious. Around gold paper, accented by berries, gold ribbon adds glitter (OPPOSITE). A one-color scheme (ABOVE) looks stunning when it includes a variety of sizes, shapes, and textures. (OVERLEAF, LEFT) A beautiful box needs just some faux fruit and gold ribbon. (OVERLEAF, RIGHT) Layer scraps of fabric and ribbon for a simple beauty.

GIFT WRAP DOESN'T HAVE to be limited to paper. Fabric bags work well, and if you like to sew, they're easy to make and a clever way to use up remnants. Even a square of fabric (or a kitchen towel, or a holiday-print hand towel) can double as gift wrap: Set the present in the middle, gather up the loose ends and secure it with a ribbon. Dramatic looks appeal to kids of all ages. For little children, the size of the package is often more important than the size of the present, so go ahead and choose oversized boxes. Whoever said "Good things come in small packages" was not under the age of 8!

(continued on page 57)

IT TAKES ONLY a moment and a metallic pen to personalize an unusual gift tag—here, a sand dollar and a glass ornament—that will become a keepsake for the recipient's tree in years to come. Other possibilities: bits of driftwood or seashells, large buttons, wooden thread spools, cookie cutters, wooden cut-outs from the craft store.

PRETTY PRESENTS

For a gift that's special from the outside in, embellish the wrapping with a decoration that makes the present pretty and becomes a keepsake itself. Match the wrapping to the recipient's personality: Kids adore boxes wrapped in comic papers or decorated with stickers of favorite fictional characters; a sports fan might get a kick out of a collage of baseball cards or sports-magazine clippings. For a seamstress, tie bias binding or rickrack around the package—or even a fabric measuring tape.

I frequently thread a tree ornament onto the package's ribbon, sometimes personalized so it serves as a gift tag, too. You can also include a package topper that hints at the contents within. With a cookbook, for instance, it's fun to tie on a cookie cutter, whisk, or wooden spoon. Choose hair bows or grosgrain ribbons for a wearer of braids; fasten a rattle or pacifier to a baby's first Christmas gift. For a present of finely milled soap or special lotions, tie a bath puff instead of a bow on the box. For an aspiring artist, set colored pencils or markers on the box in the shape of the person's initials, then tape them in place.

For gifts tags, there are numerous possibilities: photocopy baby pictures or yearbook photos for "remember-when" visual tags. Trace or photocopy initials or monograms from old books onto traditional manila tags. Rubber stamp letters work well, too.

Laura
Sara

RED RIBBONS— some plain, some dotted—twist around a tabletop tree for a nearly instant garland (OPPOSITE). The little sleigh holds an assortment of small wrapped gifts for unexpected visitors.

THE NEXT TIME you order Chinese food, request a few unused carryout containers, or look for them at a restaurant supply shop. Then, dress them with brightly colored ribbons and handmade labels and tags (LEFT).

WITH A SNIPPET of ribbon, stemware stands ready for holiday cheer (ABOVE). Choose a different color of ribbon for each glass (guests will be less likely to lose track of their beverages). Trim ribbon ends at an angle for a V-cut finish.

EVEN DOORKNOBS can be dressed up (OPPOSITE)—just make sure the bow doesn't interfere with turning the knob.

RIBBON ACCENTS

I guess it would be fair to say I'm crazy about ribbon of all kinds. A bit of ribbon is such an easy way to add holiday flair, and the choices are so varied: velvet, satin, grosgrain, silk, sheer, plain, or printed, with beaded or looped edges. Twirly ribbons shot through with metallic threads are glitzy accents for a formal mantel; gingham bows look just right for a country Christmas. One of my favorites is wire-edge ribbon, because it's so easy to get a pretty-looking bow that obediently keeps its form even when simply tied "shoestring" style. Try these ribbon tips:

Trail a length of wide ribbon along a mantel or place it as a runner down the center of the dining room table to visually link together different decorations. Give a holiday spirit to ordinary objects—flower pots, baskets, kitchen canisters, magazine racks—by garnishing them with ribbon. Perk up kitchen cabinet knobs with ribbon curls or bows. Wrap matching or contrasting lengths of ribbon around sets of silverware for a buffet. White posts spiraled with red ribbon look like peppermint sticks. Top a Christmas tree with an oversized bow, with several ribbon "tails" cascading down. Weave ribbon in and out of chair spindles or tie a large bow to the back of each chair. On Christmas day, as ribbons and bows come flying off presents, tie them on to Christmas tree branches.

(continued from page 47)

Almost every year, at least one gift is too large or awkward to wrap, a bicycle or a lamp, for example. Rather than waste rolls of paper (and precious patience), it's fun to hide the present and leave a first clue—beautifully wrapped in a decoy box—under the tree. Children enjoy the excitement of treasure hunts with clues leading them from room to room.

GRANDMOTHER'S SEWING BOX yielded the ornaments for a whimsical tree (ABOVE). A wrought-iron candle cathedral holds a four-wick candle and some fresh cedar. Cranberries in water bring a new dimension to floating candles (OPPOSITE).

AN ASYMMETRICAL ARRANGEMENT of plump candleholders on a bookcase is a nice contrast to the graceful lines of the six-taper wall sconce above (OVERLEAF).

THE ALLURE OF CANDLES

CANDLES PLAY A SPECIAL ROLE at Christmas, both for the symbolism of light banishing the dark of winter and for their own inherent romance. Tapers look just as pretty in traditional star-shaped glass holders as they did on your mother's table years ago; if the candle wiggles in the holder, anchor it with a bit of putty on the bottom or by wrapping a thin strip of foil or plastic wrap around the base. Let your imagination guide you to create new candle displays, too. For a dramatic centerpiece, group white pillar candles in varying heights and diameters to suggest the turrets and towers of a castle. If you're handy with tools, drill candle-sized holes in

a split log (birch is pretty) for a natural candle holder; or insert short tapers into cored apples. To fashion an abundant table decoration, start with a thick styrofoam circle from the craft store. Make hollows for the candles, then work with florist picks and assorted seasonal ingredients—small glass ornaments, pinecones, fresh greenery, pepper berries, cinnamon sticks, candy canes, whole nutmegs—to cover the styrofoam.

Floating candles have their own unique charm, one that is at its most potent during the holidays. They look good on all types of tables, from the dining room to living room and family room. In a large glass bowl, team them with some floating flowers or a small toy boat filled with little Christmas ornaments. For variety, tint the water with a few drops of blue or green coloring, or fill the dish with cranberries before adding water and candles.

GLASS-BEADED FRUIT becomes more treasured each year (ABOVE). I arrange the fruit between pillar candles on the mantel, at eye level and out of harm's way.

SILVER BALLS in a hurricane glass candle holder magnify the flame's shimmer (RIGHT). Picot-edged satin ribbon swirls about the arrangement.

TALL, SKINNY TAPERS are a fun change of pace. Insert several into a container filled with sand, or anchor them with a florist's "frog" and fill the container with small glass balls, marbles, or colored pebbles to conceal the frog. To intensify the light of the flames, set the candles in front of a mirror to double the amount of light given off. Other shiny surfaces—a polished silver tray, metal pitcher, glittery ornaments, especially windows at night—bounce the light back too.

CANDLES CAN EVEN BE DISPLAYED and lit in a fireplace, letting you bask in the glow of real flame with considerably less effort than chopping, splitting and stacking wood, and kindling a log fire. Choose chunky pillar candles, and set them on a tiered holder—think auditorium risers for candles—to maximize the effect. You can purchase a holder specially designed for this purpose or improvise one with a low plant stand or boards set on stacks of bricks. For safety's sake, sweep the hearth and surrounding area first.

ANOTHER CANDLELIGHT CUSTOM, whose popularity is growing in many communities, is the luminaria. These outdoor lights are simple, economical, and lovely. Candles, usually votives, are set in paper bags that have been partially filled with sand. The bags can be absolutely unadorned or fancied up with scissor snips that let the light spill out in a lacy pattern.

IN THIS CANDLE ORNAMENT, heat rising from the flames sends the angels spinning, ringing a chime each time they gently tap it in their circular journey.

TRANSLUCENT SNOWFLAKES dance across my kitchen windows, enlivening the decor inside and out (OVERLEAF).

A HOLIDAY IN EVERY ROOM

PEOPLE TEND TO CONCENTRATE holiday decorations in the living room or family room—wherever the tree is. That's a great place to start, but it's also so much fun to spread the joy throughout the whole house and to introduce decorative touches where they're least expected. How about a sprig of mistletoe in the hall closet? Or red ribbon bows tied around the coat hangers? Wisps of lace, sprigs of holly, and even tree ornaments all look wonderful attached to picture frames around the house.

WE SPEND SO MUCH TIME in the kitchen during November and December, baking holiday treats and planning meals for larger than usual groups. Judiciously selected decorative accents can boost holiday spirits as we mix another batch of cookie dough or write out yet another shopping list. Certainly we don't want to clutter the already crowded counters with fragile ornaments or holiday knickknacks; that would be counterproductive, if you'll excuse the pun. But almost certainly there's a blank spot on the wall or in the pantry, or perhaps there is an everyday picture that you wouldn't mind storing for a month or so. A wall basket, fashioned with a flat side to rest against the wall, is just the thing. You may want to get more than one because they are so versatile. Fill them with candy canes, unlit candles, or an arrangement of dried or silk flowers. Fresh flowers, always a pretty lift, can be used if the basket is lined with plastic.

HUNG IN A PROMINENT SPOT, a colorful wall basket (OPPOSITE) brightens the busiest room of the house.

WREATHS TIED to the banister (ABOVE) are a jolly change of pace from the more common garland of greenery.

TAKE ADVANTAGE OF KITCHEN windows. Many of us spend a lot of time standing at the sink, which is typically positioned in front of a window. On traditional double-hung windows, the lock makes a great spot for hanging an ornament or even a

small wreath; the sill can hold little figurines or candles. And what about that art gallery, occasionally referred to as a refrigerator? Ask your children or grandchildren to supply some Christmas masterpieces. One friend has tempera paintings her children made when they were youngsters; even though they're now grown, she always brings out these charming artworks to grace the refrigerator.

IN THE BEDROOMS, a few simple red and green accents—a touch of fresh greenery, a pot or two of flowering bulbs, some red or gingham bows, pillow shams in holiday colors—keep the ambience serene, not "busy." And instead of stashing all those beautifully wrapped presents in the closet, set out one or two small lovely gifts to serve as decorations.

I EVEN DECORATE the powder room, though not so elaborately as the rest of the house. You need little more than some red and green shaped soaps or holiday hand towels for just a touch of the mood. A scented candle, lit when company comes, keeps the air fragrant. One good friend always hangs a wreath on her powder room door to help guests identify it instead of walking into the closet alongside.

A BED POST BOUQUET comes as an unexpected flourish (OPPOSITE). Every bedroom in our house has holiday decorations of some kind, all the better to invite dreams of sugarplums.

ONE OF LIFE'S little luxuries that's worth making time for during the holidays: Breakfast in bed (ABOVE).

TYING RIBBONS present-style around their covers lets even everyday throw pillows get into the holiday spirit. Worried that an antique chair is too delicate for heavy sitters? If it's not practical to remove the chair from the room, pile it with books or even a live plant. Here, a feathery Norfolk Island pine adds some holiday greenery, but discourages sitting.

FOR HOLIDAY GUESTS

Welcome an overnight visitor to a room that you have decorated in seasonal spirit. Some easy ideas:

Instead of just plopping a set of folded bath towels on the bed, tie them with a ribbon bow. *Include a selection of light holiday-theme material: magazines, a personal stereo with a couple cassettes of Christmas carols, a video of* Miracle on 34th Street, *or O'Henry's classic "Gift of the Magi."* *Bring a poinsettia, miniature pine tree, or other plant into the room. If the plant is sturdy enough, hang a couple of tiny ornaments from the branches.* *On the pillow, leave a small dish or basket filled with peppermint drops and individually wrapped holiday chocolates.* *Is there a desk in the room? Stock it with a few holiday greeting cards and a metallic gel pen in Christmas green or red.* *If youngsters are visiting, fill a basket with children's books (the library is a good source if you don't have any), crayons or washable markers, a pad of paper or Christmas coloring book, and a sheet or two of holiday stickers.* *If the guests are annual visitors, leave in their room an album with photos from last year's celebration, together with a disposable camera for this year's fun.* *For visiting pets, loosely wrap modest presents in plenty of tissue paper; cats and dogs all enjoy batting around the package to ferret out what lies within the paper.*

Glorious Christmas
SONGBOOK

POWDER ROOMS deserve a holiday lift, too (OPPOSITE). Freesia and eucalyptus in a wall-mounted vase holder sweeten the air naturally; embroidered towels bring holiday flair to a sinkside necessity.

A MOUNTAIN LAUREL GARLAND spills out over the top of the mirror (LEFT). Pull the ends of ribbon through glass ornament loops for a change of pace from tasseled or plain ends.

The Christmas Hearth

PEOPLE WHO ARE OTHERWISE quite content with just their central heating do sometimes find themselves yearning for a fireplace at Christmas time, and there is undeniable seasonal pull to "the blazing Yule before us" and "chestnuts roasting on an open fire." If you're lucky enough to have a fireplace, definitely play up its significance at this time of year. One of the easiest ways to dress it is to lay bunches of evergreen boughs across the mantel. Scatter pinecones, large and small, natural or touched with a bit of gold paint, along the boughs. A vase filled with holly branches adds height to the display. To complete the look, flank the holly with a couple of red candles. Go even more elaborate, as you like, by combining different leaves and other natural items to create a surface full of texture. If the fireplace is used frequently, push the greenery and flowers back from the mantel's edge to prevent drying out. Spritz the greens with water from time to time.

IN HOMES WITH TODDLERS or visiting grandchildren, the mantel is the perfect spot for a ceramic Nativity set, Christmas village, or other delicate treasures that should be seen and not disturbed. Seasonal theme collections—antique Santas, handcrafted angels, snow globes, Christmas teacups—get shown to good advantage on this shelf as well. You could also choose favorite photographs from Christmases past to frame and display on the mantel, together with pieces of family silver and other heirlooms.

IN OUR HOME, the formal mantel receives the most sophisticated decorations (OPPOSITE), featuring gilded lemon leaves, stems of tiny gold balls, and mauve-toned ornaments.

A WHITE-ON-WHITE decorating scheme suggests the purity of the true Christmas spirit (OVERLEAF, LEFT). To keep the mood from seeming too cool, this room has plenty of greenery—an herbal garland, a fresh wreath, and miniature potted Norfolk Island pines—and a cozy fire in the hearth.

PINE BOUGHS snipped from the backyard are simply laid on top of a cupboard or mantel (OVERLEAF RIGHT). Red pepper berries and a striped peppermint stick peek out of the knit white stocking.

IRE

A GIFT OF PROMISE

At Christmas, paper white narcissus bulbs (the plant behind the teddy bears opposite) are one of the easiest, most gratifying flowering plants to grow at home. From drab bulbs that look more or less like tiny onions, regular watering, and a bit of sunshine, a graceful arrangement of tall, slender green stems topped with delicate, intensely fragrant flowers springs forth within a few weeks' time, almost like magic.

Here's how: Fill a shallow bowl or flowerpot with pebbles and nestle a few bulbs into the dish, making a slight depression in the pebbles for each, then mounding up pebbles around base to steady bulbs. Add water to just reach the base of the bulbs. In about two weeks, a mass of skinny, tenacious roots will emerge from the bottom of the bulb and anchor it in place, and green shoots will begin to poke out of the top. Add water as necessary to keep the roots, but not the bulb, wet.

About two weeks later, the blossoms appear. If the stems get very leggy, you may need to support them by inserting a long dowel or something similar into the pebbles and tying the stems on with a soft ribbon or strip of fabric, similar to the way you would stake up a tomato. Expect the blossoms to last about two weeks. As a hostess gift, present the bulbs in the pebbled dish, with instructions to water four to five weeks before blooms are desired.

BROTHERLY BEARS "Honey" and "Teddy," dressed snugly in their Christmas woolens, are stationed alongside the fireplace. After packing the back of their sleigh with ivy and poinsettia, they've jumped on board, ready for a ride.

"God Bless Us Every One"

Seasonal rituals repeated each year bring the comfort and delight of familiarity and rekindle memories for young and old alike. Many families enjoy Christmas customs so firmly established that no one can remember exactly how they began. Traditions have to start somewhere, however, so if you try something new that your family really loves, do it next year and voilà! A tradition has been born.

Will and I foster traditions we hope will let our boys grow up with a deep sense of the meaning of Christmas and the joy of the holiday's just-for-fun aspects, too. On December 24th, Will reads from the Book of Luke, in an updated, conversational version of the Bible so Gene and Jeff understand the story of the first Christmas. The boys each have a Nativity, ready for endless role playing for the figurines—the Wise Men diving from the stable roof; the donkey and the camel butting heads—but somehow the figures always end up circled around the baby Jesus.

A family carol sing is important to our celebration, too; then we set out Santa's snack and hang the stockings. Our older son is at the age when he questions Santa's reality, raising the anxiety of his younger brother. We answer their concerns with reassurances: "Santa is just as real as we pretend him to be"—which at our house, is very, very real indeed!

CHARLES DICKENS'S *A Christmas Carol*, set in Victorian England, still resonates with readers today (ABOVE). Who can fail to respond to the poignancy of a heart touched and forever changed by the spirit of Christmas?

THIS CRÈCHE, a very special holiday accessory in our family, is an heirloom in the making (OPPOSITE). A touch of fresh greenery completes the Nativity scene.

GLORIA

Of all the ornaments and details that bring charm and grace to the holiday home, it's the Christmas tree that most enchants and captivates young and old alike

Christmas Tree Magic

SUDDENLY, THE CHRISTMAS SPIRIT is here in earnest, with the arrival of that big green evergreen perfuming the air and waiting to be decked out splendidly with lights, garlands, bows, shiny balls, candy canes. It's only a matter of time before tantalizing presents pile up underneath. No other single holiday element transforms the mood of the home so instantly and thoroughly. Children are absolutely swept away by the very idea of a tree—an actual tree!—inside the house. Even those of us who have seen at least a few dozen Christmases can't help but pause and smile.

OUR CHRISTMAS season begins the day after Thanksgiving, when we trim the tree. Holiday decorating is much more fun and relaxing when done at our leisure before December even gets underway. We then have a whole month to enjoy and appreciate our handiwork.

THE SWEETLY diminutive miniature trees stationed all through the house make nice "satellites" to the family's main tree. Smaller trees bring the chance for trying more than one decorating style or showcasing a prized collection of very special ornaments. A little personalized tree makes a thoughtful gift, too. Suspend bulbs of garlic from pink ribbons for an avid cook; for a gardener, dried flowers. And any grandmother would be tickled by a family tree, adorned with family photos in miniature frames. These trees could also be sent to faraway relatives or anyone in a nursing home or a hospital.

A FOREST OF TREES

ALL EVERGREENS ARE NOT ALIKE, as any parent who has ever visited a tree farm with excited children can tell you. Commercial tree growers raise more than a dozen varieties of evergreens in the United States for sale as Christmas trees, and the choice of branches that are airy or densely packed, short- or long-needled is a matter of personal preference. I look for a perfect, symmetrical Christmas tree shape, one that is evenly balanced all around. Keep in mind that a tree with an open branch configuration that might look too "loose" in the forest will be filled in with ornaments; on the other hand, a lush tree with tightly spaced branches might not allow your ornaments to hang freely.

IF SOMEONE WERE TO LEAD YOU blindfolded into a room and sit you down beside a balsam tree, then instruct you to inhale deeply, the unmistakable aroma of pine would instantly make you exclaim "Christmas!" Because of its distinctive, memory-provoking fragrance, the balsam is one of the most popular varieties of Christmas trees. Its needles are short, with somewhat flat sprigs, and the branches are usually widely spaced, leaving ample room for hanging decorations. Balsams are probably the most traditional of Christmas trees, perfect for collections of vintage and antique ornaments.

THOUGH NOT BLUE LIKE THE SKY, the blue spruce definitely has a bluish, frosty cast to its green needles. The needles are a little longer and lusher than the balsam's, and the branches

tend to be similarly open and airy. Because the needles of the blue spruce can be especially sharp, be sure to wear heavy work gloves for transport and handling. White spruce, which is not really white, has bluish-green needles that are slightly shorter than those of the blue spruce. "Long-haired" Scotch pine evergreens also are very popular as holiday trees, and their full, dense shape and shaggy needles give a much softer appearance. Long wispy needles and delicate branches characterize the white pine—heavy ornaments, though, may make its branches sag.

WHEN GUESTS are on the way, Will lights a fire or, if time is short, I'll light a few candles so our guests' first glimpse into the house (OPPOSITE) will be of an inviting scene.

THINK BEYOND the expected primary-red-and-bright-green scheme. Glass ornaments in muted red and olive green, along with non-traditional hues such as purple and dusty blue (ABOVE), look elegant, especially with a subtly shimmering surface.

SETTING UP THE TREE

LOCATION. LOCATION. LOCATION. That's an old real estate adage, but it's also important when deciding where to put the Christmas tree. You need a spot away from heat sources, and close enough to an electric outlet so the lights can be plugged in easily, with cords out of the traffic pattern so no one trips. But there are aesthetic considerations, too, which I learned the hard way one year. We had chosen the perfect spot for our huge blue spruce, had it positioned in the stand—then realized that the tip of the tree came smack between two

(continued on page 94)

LIGHT STREAMS through holes punched in star-shaped bulb covers (OPPOSITE).

STRINGS OF PLUMP colored tree bulbs, popular in the 1950s and 1960s, are still sold, but lights have become an artform in themselves. Birds (TOP) and tinsel balls (ABOVE) are two pretty choices.

Christmas Lights

In addition to illuminating the tree, lighting can be put to good advantage elsewhere inside the house, too:

Light up wreaths, indoor trees, or large houseplants—even floral arrangements or the greenery lining the mantel. Light mirrors, framed landscapes, galleries of photographs and art. If plug-in strings of lights are awkward for these situations, substitute battery-powered strings. A battery-operated string could also call attention to a particularly special present under the tree, or make it possible to display an illuminated arrangement on the dining table or buffet.

Rope lights, a relative newcomer to the market, can outline stair risers, newel posts and banisters, windows, kitchen cabinets, doorway arches—you name it. The "ropes" consist of tiny clear or colored bulbs housed within a flexible clear-plastic tube.

In decades past, beaded curtains were popular for adding a touch of romance in open doorways. A modern variation, light "curtains," are best used to section off part of a room.

"Icicle" lights—horizontal wires support numerous dangling vertical sections with varying number of bulbs, to look like illuminated lace or icicles under the eaves—have become popular for outdoor decorating. Indoors, they make a pretty contribution in a bay window.

Collecting Ornaments

One of the pleasures of the season is getting all the boxes of ornaments out of storage. Peeling away the protective tissue and cotton, we relive some favorite memories as each old friend emerges. The boys feel they are getting a head start on unwrapping presents; the anticipation and excitement for this year's holiday surge again. We each have our particular favorites—some are traditional, some are not. One of Gene Colyer's prized decorations is a miniature leather cowboy hat, sent by his godmother in Texas. Cared for and displayed with love year after year, special decorations become family heirlooms.

We love adding to the collection, too. Every year, Grandmillie and Aunt Sue handcraft a special tree decoration for each family member, and Will and I give our boys an ornament, too, so they'll start their adult lives ready to trim their own trees!

In our travels throughout the year, we're always on the lookout for souvenirs that will personalize and beautify our tree. Side by side with the shimmering glass balls, our trees have included butterfly decorations purchased at the Smithsonian gift shop after a visit to the Museum of Natural History and a treasure trove of seashells gathered on annual family vacations to the Florida shore.

THESE GOLDEN and deep-burgundy egg-shaped ornaments resemble the exquisite artistry of Fabergé. Although designed to be hung, they look equally pretty off the tree, especially in the shimmer and glow of the fireplace.

THE BOYS' OWN tree is the perfect spot for them to display one-of-a-kind holiday decorations. Other children might get a kick out of attaching ribbon to favorite figurines, toy cars, or candies to turn them into ornaments. One year, when the boys were too young to create a tree on their own, I decorated a little tree with pacifiers and baby rattles!

(continued from page 89)

skylights, stealing the limelight from the angel. So we slipped rolling casters under the massive steel tree stand, tied a rope around the trunk, and pulled it as if it were a little wagon over to the other side of the room! It worked, and it's all pretty funny in retrospect, but it definitely proves that Step One is to visualize the finished scene.

BEFORE YOU GET TO THE DECORATING stage of "trimming," you'll face the first task of trimming, that is, slicing off at least an inch from the bottom of the tree. Don't throw away any lower branches you remove while you're making the tree fit in the stand; consider them a bonus. Secure a bunch of the branches with twine or wire, then tie them up with a big ribbon bow for a quick, pretty door decoration; arrange them in and among mantel decorations; fill vases and pieces of art pottery with arrangements of branches and stems of holly, winterberry, or bittersweet; or tuck branches into a pretty basket along with some pinecones and Christmas ornaments. Evergreen branches bring holiday cheer to a vase of roses or lilies, and give the display a more festive look.

THE TWINKLING LIGHTS

THE TRADITION OF CELEBRATING Christmas with a lighted tree is thought to date back to Germany in the mid-1600s, when the Protestant reformer Martin Luther put candles on an evergreen in his home to re-create for his family the wonder

Jeffrey
Jeffrey
sus is the light for...
Jeffrey

he had felt at the beauty of a forest under a starlit sky. In America, the Christmas-tree tradition gained widespread popularity in the mid-1800s, with lighted candles wired to the branches—very dramatic yet very dangerous! A bucket of water was the era's must-have decorating accessory. But the earliest electric tree lights were no picnic either, as the wiring required all the bulbs to operate in order to complete the circuit. When one bulb burned out, none of the bulbs would light up, necessitating testing a fresh replacement in each socket until the culprit was identified. Talk about adding stress to the holiday season! Fortunately, a more sensible wiring configuration eliminated this problem decades ago.

UNTIL THE YEAR we brought home a blue spruce, I never quite understood the importance of the interplay between the color of the needles and the cast of the light. My sweet little white lights somehow just didn't create the right look. I discovered some lovely lights resembling small chamberstick candles, and suddenly the entire tree was perfect.

THE CHOICES FOR TREE LIGHTS are absolutely mind-boggling these days. In addition to the chunky colorful bulbs that have been around for decades, lights now come in almost every conceivable form—seasonal motifs such as stars, snowflakes, and Santa faces; pink roses, opalescent pearls, and faceted bulbs that resemble jewels; even chili peppers, farm animals, and favorite cartoon characters! With so many choices, lighting becomes an integral element in the overall mood of the tree, from formal elegance to down-home country to

LIVE TREES ARE thirsty; they will last longest if you make sure they get enough to drink. Since the fresh cut will "scar" over within a short time after being sawed, preventing water from being absorbed, it's important to recut a thin slice from the trunk as soon as the tree is home. Put it in water immediately, and make sure the water level remains above the cut end of the trunk. Use a sturdy stand and be sure the tree is completely secured before putting up any decorations.

EVERY TREE has a different personality. This just-for-fun white spruce, decorated with snowmen and a red wooden apple garland, represents the lighter side of the season. Logs around the tree's base substitute for the tree skirt that would typically wrap a tree indoors. The skirt tradition began in the days of candlelit trees, when a sturdy cloth would be set on the floor to catch the dripping wax. Before long, decorated tree skirts were being sold commercially. Later, skirts helped to conceal unattractive tree stands.

playful humor. Many of the lights I adore don't really work stylistically on my tree, so I'll use them instead to light an entryway or to wrap around the birdhouse. It's fun to use strings of Christmas lights as impromptu decorations around the house; they can bring to rooms some of the glow of candlelight without any of its danger.

WHEN SETTING OUT TO LIGHT the tree, take a good, hard look at the branch structure before you begin. Trees with densely packed branches are easiest to work with; you need to do little more than wind the light strings around the tree and through the boughs. If the branches are very open and airy, you may need to conceal the wire a little more effectively. Start at the trunk, run the wire out along a branch, clip a bulb to the branch's tip, run it back toward the trunk, then continue on with another branch until you have the number of lights you want on the tree. Even if your tree is in a corner or up against a wall, try to arrange the lights evenly across the branches and up and down the tree. Always evenly distribute lights over a tree visible through the living room window, for that is a wonderful sight at Christmas.

BEGIN WITH PLENTY of extension cords and adapters, and organize wiring so that it is all tucked safely out of sight behind the tree, where no one will trip over it. Be certain to check the manufacturer's recommendations regarding the number of light strings and extensions that can be used together. Once the lights have been strung, adjusted, and deemed perfect, the ornaments come out of their boxes and the real fun begins.

Snow
JINGLE
FRIENDS

FINISHING TOUCHES

ALL THAT GLITTERS is not necessarily good—but some of it is great. Use just enough shiny surfaces to reflect the lights of the tree, to add an undeniably magic shimmer, especially when the tree is the only illumination in an otherwise dark room—whether your glittery touch consists of garlands of gold beads, dozens of sparkly glass ornaments, or even lengths of silver ribbon swagged from branch to branch.

ONCE THE ORNAMENTS ARE HUNG, bring the whole look together with a unifying detail. Christopher Radko, famous for his popular Christmas ornaments, makes lovely cookie ornaments: Shape the dough with cookie cutters, then cut out the center portion with a smaller cutter of the same shape. Place the cookies on a baking tray and fill the center openings with different colors of crushed hard candy; with a knife poke a hole at the top center of each cookie. During baking, the hard candy melts, and the cooled cookies resemble stained glass. Slip thin ribbon through the holes and hang the cookies on the tree. Cookies used for ornaments or display, though, should not be eaten.

ON CHRISTMAS EVE afternoon the boys and I always sit beneath the magical tree and share a favorite holiday story (OPPOSITE), all of us knowing that Saint Nick will soon arrive.

CHRISTMAS SPIES: The temptation to peek is just too great (BELOW), especially with a co-conspirator in the next bed.

Gene

At last, Christmas is here!
Revel in the joy of being home for the holidays,
together with the people closest to your heart

JOY AT HOME

DECEMBER TWENTY-FIFTH. OUTSIDE THE MORNING dawns quietly but inside, the stillness has already given way to shining wide eyes, gleeful voices, and plenty of hugs as the boys, bursting with excitement, bounce into our room ready to dive into the celebration. Today is the culmination of all the planning, giggling, wrapping, baking, decorating, and, of course, whispered conspiracies.

Let me take a brief moment for a reality check here. By the time Christmas arrives, incredible anticipation has built up for the children, while the adults in all likelihood have

MARK EACH PLACE at a formal dinner with a beautiful still life assembled on a bread-and-butter plate. A Christmas rose, nestled in evergreen and teamed with a berry sprig and a fresh pear, sets off the picture-frame name card.

A CANDLE IN A GRANNY JAR infuses the buffet with a delicious whiff of strawberry-raspberry (ABOVE). The sunny lemons accent a simple plate stand of red and green apples.

ON CHRISTMAS MORNING, breakfast tends to come rather late for us. If I have time, I'll make a coffee cake; if not, rather than fuss with cooking eggs or pancakes, we set out purchased pastries and fresh fruit (OPPOSITE).

been running around crazily to create the perfect holiday. Everybody's routine is slightly out of whack, so you can expect a few bumps along the way. To keep the family on an even keel and make sure this time is actually enjoyable and not superstressed, be realistic about what you can do, stay flexible for last-minute changes, and keep your sense of humor close by. Having children has definitely changed my holiday expectations and priorities. Our celebration dinners have become more casual, less reliant upon elaborate last-minute preparations. I have come to embrace shortcuts such as purchasing some of the meal rather than feeling I must personally handcraft every last morsel of food. With children in your home, you can't help but re-experience the magic of Christmas newly discovered. This is their day, and I for one don't intend to miss a single moment with them.

FINAL FLOURISHES

STILL, I FIND THERE ARE LOTS of quick touches—none of which takes more than a couple of minutes—that collectively enhance the visual beauty of the celebration. When it's time for our family meal, for instance, I want the table to look both welcoming and elegant—but not intimidating—to reflect our mood of celebration and family togetherness. Candles are a given, as is choosing a favorite tablecloth and setting out some special-occasion tureens and the good china. Those details alone convey the message of the importance of

(continued on page 110)

HAPPY
IS THE
HOME
THAT
SHELTERS
A
FRIEND

MISS SHARI'S APPLE CRISP

This homestyle dessert, shared by my dear friend Shari Miller, is perfect for our on-the-go family because it's easy to make and so delicious. It's yummy warm from the oven, crowned with cinnamon whipped cream. I love the fact that I can make the dessert a day ahead, underbaking it slightly and then refrigerating it until a last-minute reheat. A colorful holiday variation is a handful or two of fresh cranberries along with the apples.

FILLING:

5 Granny Smith apples, peeled, cored, and cut into 1/4-inch slices

1/4 cup granulated sugar

1 tsp. fresh lemon juice

1 tsp. cinnamon

CRUMB TOPPING:

1 cup all-purpose flour

1/2 cup (1 stick) unsalted butter, melted

1/2 cup light brown sugar

1/4 tsp. salt

1 Tbs. cinnamon

CINNAMON WHIPPED CREAM:

1 pint heavy cream

1/4 cup granulated sugar

1 Tbs. cinnamon

1. To make the filling, preheat the oven to 350°. Generously butter a 10-inch glass or metal pie plate. In a large bowl, toss the apples with the sugar, lemon juice, and cinnamon. Transfer the mixture to the prepared pie plate.
2. To make the crumb topping, in a medium bowl, combine all the topping ingredients with your fingertips or a pastry blender until the mixture resembles coarse meal. Sprinkle evenly over the apples.
3. Bake for about 1 hour, or until the apples are very tender when a knife is inserted in the center of the crisp.
4. To make the whipped cream, in the bowl of an electric mixer, combine the heavy cream, sugar, and cinnamon. With the whisk attachment, beat the mixture at high speed until the cream forms soft peaks. Do not overbeat.
5. Serve the crisp warm, with the whipped cream.

SERVES 5 TO 6

THE RECIPE CAN BE DOUBLED AND BAKED IN A 9- BY 13-INCH PAN

MISS JOAN'S ENGLISH COOKIES

My mother's English shortbread cookies never fail to bring a flood of emotions. Transporting me to my very earliest memories, the heavenly aroma as they bake is, to me, the quintessential fragrance of Christmas. For pretty cookies, score the pan lengthwise at 1½-inch intervals. Next, make diagonal crosswise cuts to form diamonds. The cookies are light, crisp, lovely. They freeze well, too, so I can bake them before the season gets too hectic.

1 cup (2 sticks) unsalted butter at room temperature

1 cup granulated sugar

1 large egg yolk

1 tsp. vanilla extract

2 cups all-purpose flour

1 cup finely chopped pecans

1. Preheat the oven to 350°. Using the paddle attachment of an electric mixer, cream the butter and sugar on medium speed until light and fluffy, about 5 minutes. Scrape the bowl several times during mixing.
2. Add the egg yolk and vanilla and beat until the mixture is well blended and light in color.
3. On low speed, gradually beat in the flour. The dough will come together into a ball on the paddle. (At this point, the dough can be wrapped tightly in plastic and frozen for up to one month; defrost before shaping.)
4. With your fingertips, spread the dough in a thin layer about ¼-inch thick on an unbuttered jelly roll pan. Do not push the dough onto the sides.
5. Sprinkle the dough with the chopped pecans and very lightly press in.
6. Bake for 20 to 25 minutes, until the sides are golden brown.
7. Let the cookies cool on the baking sheet on a rack for 5 to 10 minutes.
8. Using a sharp knife, cut the cookies into diamonds.

YIELD: ABOUT 3 DOZEN 2-INCH COOKIES

(continued from page 104)

the day. Children past the spilling stage will get a thrill out of "fancy" drinks: milk or apple juice served in a grown-up goblet!

Personalized place cards are fun, too, even for a small get-together. My collection of miniature silver frames can hold name tags or a small photo of each guest; your budding artists can decorate folded heavy paper with scalloped-edged scissors, holiday stickers, or cutouts from decorative hole punches. I sometimes take this idea a step further and create a "place piece"—sort of an individual centerpiece that's part seasonal decoration, part name tag. Start with a bread plate or a glass custard cup and build a little tableau with a sprig of greens, a fresh or silk flower, a Christmas ornament or two. Feel free to combine saucers from various china sets or one-of- a-kind candy dishes. You could also outfit each place with a small basket filled with petite fruits (lady apples, kumquats, seckel pears, grapes, baby bananas) or a miniature box of chocolates tied with a ribbon. Offer children "bouquets" of red and green lollipops or a few gold-foil-wrapped coins gathered in a square of velvet that's tied with a ribbon. For three or four toddlers, cut the picture from a Christmas card into as many puzzle-shaped pieces as there are children and let the kids solve the puzzle.

I TUCK SOME FRESH GREENS into the holly berry napkin ring (ABOVE). Our green and gold wedding china is perfect for Christmas.

A SPARKLING BRASS candlestick makes a beautiful pedestal for a cascade of pepper berries and preserved ivy leaves (OPPOSITE). The secret is a styrofoam anchor inserted into the hollow of the candlestick.

A TINY NOSEGAY of lemon leaves and pearlescent "berries" tied with a shimmery sheer ribbon dresses up dining room chairs (OPPOSITE). Wire-edged ribbon holds the bouquet in shape, but you can also secure the stems with a rubber band or a bit of thin wire before adding the ribbon.

EXTRA HOLLY BERRY napkin rings double as "bracelets" for the chandelier candles (LEFT). Pots of tiny cedars introduce another element of seasonal green, which is repeated once more on the wall ledge.

A KISSING BALL is tied to the chandelier with gingham ribbon (OVERLEAF).

TABLE DRESS-UPS

While it's a good idea to choose low dining table centerpieces that won't prevent guests from seeing each other, sideboards and buffet tables are good spots for a vertical showpiece. Some ideas:

Select a well-formed tree branch from the yard and spray-paint it white or silver. Set it into a vase or a marble-filled jar and decorate it with red and silver glass ornaments. Dress a teddy bear or any stuffed animal in a Christmas outfit, easily improvised by cutting a length of red fabric and fringing the ends to serve as a scarf, or simply tying on a festive bow tie from holiday ribbon. Don't forget a cap with a jingle bell or two on its tip. Suspend snowflake ornaments or origami cranes folded from shiny paper or squares of foil gift wrap over the table with various lengths of ribbon. Stack a tower of several beautifully wrapped presents (even if the boxes are actually empty). Cover a large styrofoam cone (available at craft stores) with holiday-print fabric or lengths of wide ribbon. Wind a silver or gold elastic cord in a spiral around the "tree" to mimic a garland, then tuck in candy canes or red and green lollipops. Line a set of baskets with red-checked kitchen towels or Christmas napkins and decorate the handles with star garlands or big ribbon bows. Heap each basket with a selection of pinecones, nuts, or assorted fruits. Fill a jam jar with jumbo candy canes.

MY THREE-TIERED plate stand works beautifully as a table-top conversation piece, too. This arrangement took less than ten minutes to put together: I chose some pieces from my collections of beaded fruits and whimsical ornaments and placed them on the stand, securing some of the smaller pieces as necessary with bits of putty. A plaid taffeta tablecloth mirrors the colors of the fruit, giving a little more warmth than the glass table underneath. A few lengths of sheer ribbon cascade from the top.

TIED WITH A WIDE chocolate-colored ribbon, a silver tray looks for all the world like a glorious present. What a beautiful way to offer an after-dinner treat! The ribbon, angle-cut for a smart finish, is perfect here because its wire holds the shape of the bow and the position of the tails.

Relax and Celebrate!

SOONER OR LATER ON CHRISTMAS DAY—preferably sooner—it's time to say "Enough!" However far we've gotten in last-minute decorative touches will suffice. Now we can turn our full attention to the pleasure of sharing the holiday within the loving circle of family. Although my two brothers and I have long since left the shelter of our parents' Kentucky home, we all get together for a huge celebration each Christmas. It's such a treat for our sons Gene and Jeff to celebrate the holiday with their grandparents, Uncle Gene, Aunt Lucy and cousins Jenny and Christy, Uncle Jeff, Aunt Peggy and cousin Christopher, Aunt Mary, Uncle Kevin and cousin Joe.

THE YOUNGEST GENERATION so much enjoy playing together, establishing their own cousin traditions and favorite games. There's tremendous excitement as wrapping paper comes flying off and new toys are admired and shared. Throughout the festivities, as we feast and exchange gifts, we try never to lose sight of the true meaning of the holiday, the original Gift, God's son. He's the real reason for Christmas.

WEARY BUT CONTENT, THE DAY winding to a close, we can at last simply sit and enjoy the sheer pleasure of just being together as a family. The children will plead for another moment or so to play with their new toys in the glow of the Christmas tree lights, then upstairs we'll go for a bedtime story, prayers, and a few last whispers about a very special day that will stay always in our hearts.

ACKNOWLEDGMENTS

SO MANY PEOPLE played essential roles in the creation of this book, and to them I offer my heartfelt thanks:

Jill Cohen and her associates Ellen Bruzelius, Sarah Butterworth, and Cassandra Reynolds at QVC Publishing initiated this project and brought all the right people to work on the book. I am so grateful to John Smallwood and Ella Stewart for bringing photographer Jeff McNamara and his assistant Jessica Williams, stylist Ingrid Leess, and writer Mary Caldwell onto our team. They are responsible for so much of what is good about this book.

The vendor families with whom it is our privilege to work made many of the beautiful items you see in these pages, specifically, Donna and Burt Hanna, Lee and Joe Williams, Annett Davidson, Helen and Raymond Wong, Linda Smith, Darcy Bartsch, Linda and George de Bruin, Holly and David Whitney, Kevin Mitchell, Kaye Connell, Mary and Don Haldeman, Frieda and Dan Hanley, Carol and Tom Bouquet, Ann and Kirk Lineweaver, Steve Conant, Mel Lidstone, Hans Hollerbach, and Geoffrey Harris.

Friends at QVC were so supportive and helpful: Doug Briggs, Darlene Daggett, Robb Cadigan, Bill O'Donnell,

MaryBeth Warshaw, Caryn Fallon, Chris Morley, Betty Amabile, Ann Marie Schmitz, Michelle Barbacane, Maureen Kelly, Paul Colaiezzi, Nick Roseto, Rich Davis, and Kyle Brown. And Christopher Radko was kind enough to share a special holiday recipe.

Shari and Jeff Miller fed our crews and made interior modifications to our home just in time for the photography, and Mary and Will Roth grew our beautiful blue spruce.

My associates at The Valerie Parr Company—Gail Anderson, Mary Carroll, Elena Conte, Kasia Gonaciarz, Norma Kratt, and Liz Reilly—worked tirelessly preparing for the book. And Margi Watters did a great job assisting with the research.

MOTHER AND DAD AND MY HUSBAND, WILL, were always there with encouragement. Thanks also, Dad, for the beautiful furniture you so lovingly crafted, and brother Gene (always ready for a road trip), for driving it up from Kentucky; brother Jeff, for Thanksgiving culinary prowess; Aunt Janet, for all the handcrafted treasures. To our sons, Gene Colyer and Jeffrey—you are the inspiration for so much of our holiday decorating and celebration.

Resources

THE FOLLOWING ARE THE ITEMS pictured in this book that are part of the Valerie Parr Hill decorative accessory collection available from QVC. To place an order, please call 1-800-345-1515 or visit us online at www.qvc.com.

Page	
10	Set of Six Autumn-Berry Mini-Wreaths H30020
20, 122	Glass Bowl with Wrought-Iron Base H64921
21	Tri-colored Eucalyptus Oval Mirror H30021
22	Autumn-Blend Berry Wreath H64916 Three-Wick Pillar Candle with Glass Plate H71110
24	Autumn Harvest Candle Collection H71111
29	Set of Six Autumn-Berry Mini-Wreaths H30020
30	Thanksgiving Wreath H29381
34	Wrought-Iron Cathedral Candle Holder H17280 Vanilla Four-Wick Fireplace Candle Refill H63906
36	Fresh Balsam-Fir Holiday Wreath H95000 Fresh Balsam & Mixed Green Swag with Bow H72432 Solid Brass Wreath Hanger with Celtic Braid H29295
39	Fresh Balsam-Fir Holiday Wreath H95000
52	Wooden Santa's Sleigh H43537

57	Wrought-Iron Cathedral Candle Holder H17280 Vanilla Four-Wick Fireplace Candle Refill H63906
58	Scroll Motif Six Taper Wall Sconce H64919 Curved Glass Hurricane H21472 Fresh Balsam & Mixed Green Swag with Bow H72432
60	Set of Twelve Vanilla Fireplace Candles H64267
66	Floral Holiday Wire Wall Basket H17289 Wrought Iron Three-Tiered Plate Stand H72477
78	Nine-Pedestal Wrought-Iron Fireplace Candelabra H72458 Set of Twelve Vanilla Fireplace Candles H64267 Wooden Santa's Sleigh H43537 Holiday Cone-Shaped Topiary H17290 Holly-Berry Holiday Wreath H64915 Fresh Balsam & Mixed Green Swag with Bow H72432
80	Wooden Santa's Sleigh H43537
83	Eleven-piece Porcelain Handpainted Nativity Set with Creche H43044
88	Fresh Balsam & Mixed Green Swag with Bow H72432
99	Fresh Balsam-Fir Holiday Wreath H95000 Wooden Holiday Snowman Sled H25934
104	Valerie's Fresh Fruit Preserves Candle H25154
105	Wrought-Iron Three-Tiered Plate Stand H72477 Set of Four Handcrafted Oval Wooden Shaker Boxes H71991 Set of Four Checkered Heart-Shaped Plates H63176
114, 124	Holiday Kissing Ball H17292 Set of Six Cranberry Mini-Wreaths H30022
116	Set of Three Glass Cake-Plate Stands H17291

And to All... Merry Christmas